ANXIETY
Paolo Russo

I edition: June 2018
© Paolo Russo
ISBN 978-0-244-99040-4
Translation by Sara Cinque

Paolo Russo

ANXIETY

"know yourself in order to heal"

Treaty of ethical analysis: metaphor and symptoms

Psylibri Edition

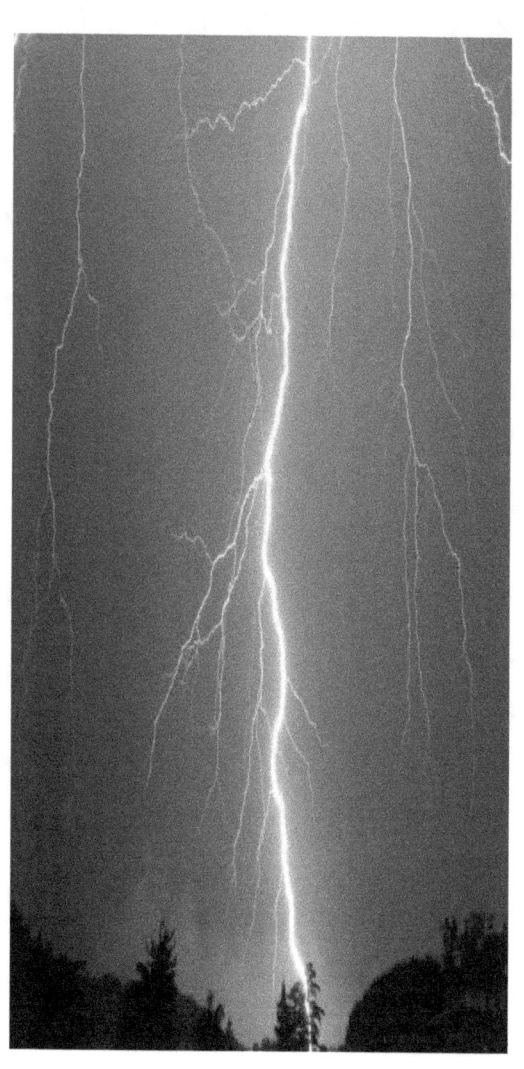

Anxiety

A fiery hug
of burning thoughts,
cries that anticipate the breath,
jarring echos along sick paths
that contaminate hopes with death.
When the stars at night, are heavy steps
on a barren land, of a dark tomorrow,
and cruel images, on golden screens,
patience becomes powerless
giving way to this live death.
Arms get open and desolate
an icy chill spreads inside the whole body
and it cripples the soul and reduces dreams
to silence...

Until the cold stops
and you begin to breath again.

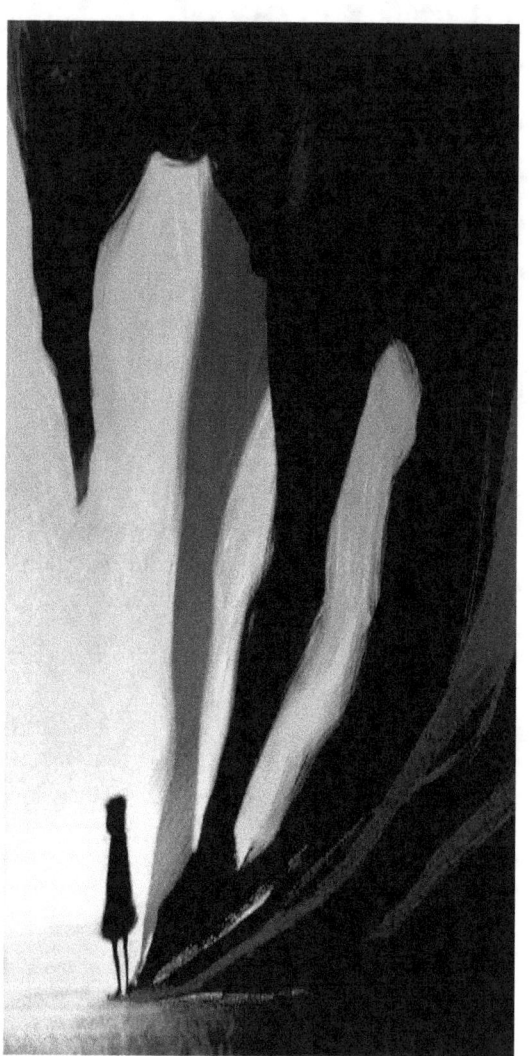

PRESENTATION

When, in your everyday life, you will find a heavy burden that doesn't make any sense, that is annoying, like a spider on your hair that you can't get off and when, after experimenting your impotence to know it, you will decide to accept it in your life... When you will get to the point of asking yourself why you, of all people, experienced this fear that disarms you, that makes you nonsensical, that makes you mean, different, weird, that's when you will deal with the difficulty of living with the urge to resist, with the urge to be different... that's when you will develop new spaces in your mind for your monsters... without even wanting to, you have begun to stitch them on yourself and only when you gave in to them you understood that the bad thoughts were cries coming from parts of you that you were suffocating and that are now at your disposal for your journey in the discovery of life's things.

This book is dedicated especially to you, you who can understand that faults are hidden wounds, fed by a feeling of visceral restlessness, they are thorns on wounded skin and on wounds that never healed. When you got mad and you wanted to break everything you were simply speaking your monster's language, you wanted to be understood, recognized, you wanted to be loved, now, as then, when you were fragile and someone stepped on your needs.

Dedicated to you, who understood that life is an amazing gift and who turned your struggle to live into a disease, for a long time, for too long... and you who built tempered walls on your wreckage, walls that sometimes were insurmountable until you understood that raising them is pointless when you are being yourself.

And darned the time that you loved someone because it is the intimacy that recreates those fears that you locked in the most hidden room of your subconscious. You, who still to this day fear the wounds, this book is dedicated to you, to you because you can understand and you can make a whole new world out of your internal journey. Painting walls of fragility with new colours, even the walls of those people who quelled their souls because they couldn't tolerate those wails, those unbearable cries.

When you write, draw, dance, play music, compose or when you give everything you've got to turn your cry into a virtue, your scars into wisdom, your presence into a safe space to allow others to smile sincerely.

You know I can't explain anxiety to you, because anxiety is a place that has to be explored. I can tell you about the anxieties that I met and about the statues of fragility on devastated squares, squares of fake self love where gods were erected. Those squares were the places of sorrow and anytime the believers gathered to worship these sculptures these ones underwent a transformation, sometimes they were becoming giant, erudite, beautiful and sometimes they were becoming nice, competent and smart, gods doomed to complacency...

Anxiety is an open entrance that leads to that world that is described by poets, that leads to what psychoanalysts call subconscious. It's a terrible place where sorrows become stabs on your heart, high falls, cracked skin, to use a poetic lexicon, yet it is a place that doesn't know death, it's death while you are still alive. It's the feeling that most resembles what common people refers to with the term "wandering soul". Those immortal wandering figures invisible to most...

Anxiety is a feeling of extreme pain, pain of representation, we are killers, mean people, we are victims of diseases but we ourselves are killed, wounded, ill, obviously with presumption, and we feel that pain that lives inside of us. It's an act of a dramatic poetry where we become actors and fabulous performers. We are the mind that doesn't know death because anxiety's distress is a distress that goes beyond death: physically we die when our body can't take it anymore, psychologically we experience going beyond endurance...

Enjoy the read

Paolo Russo
(www.drpaolorusso.it)

INTRODUCTION

The Matrix (from "I Fiumi di Jane" -*Jane's Rivers*- February 2000)
"The matrix constitutes the central core of our life. We have to look at it as a shell constantly changing according to the "debris" that are brought to the matrix itself from the rivers that constitute our life. Destiny is to be considered as a "law" that doesn't strictly fit into the typical meaning of this word, but that represents a circumstance already outlined before having it lived, even if only in the more general aspect. In fact, the situations that can occur in order to determine the upheaval of a phase of our life that is, more or less, "bad" are numerous.
The "bad phase" is determined by "agents" that negatively affect the formation or, better, the determination of a goal that has to be achieved.
This phase occurs in people who didn't have certain debris absorbed in the optimal way or even when the rivers

from which to draw experience weren't explored.

The "good phase" is constituted by those circumstances in which a certain goal can be reached through help so thanks to the influence of an external agent; this phase entails an immense joy and a formation of debris that at the end of a river's path will make, inside our matrix, a connection with the external agent that contributed to our joy.

The rivers determine situations that often change the way we interpret reality: the more we get away from our matrix, the more we see things differently, because we live the debris without having them be concomitant with the others that we already absorbed in our matrix.

It's never appropriate to live fully detached from our own matrix but, on the contrary, it's always appropriate to be guided to achieve the matrix by an agent who can be a friend, a person we trust…

The matrix, that represents the central

part of ourselves, is never to be neglected, and to do that it's appropriate to compare the life we are living now with a situation of joy. Only by doing this, it's possible to know if we are now living a river that is far from our matrix and therefore to act accordingly. When the rivers are detached from the matrix in a crucial way, it's better not to face important situations because there would be the risk of dealing with them in the wrong way.

This would lead to an even more clear detachment from what is our matrix, and if similar moments become habitual you can risk to live rivers that are significantly distant from the matrix and, therefore, you can risk to see reality different from what it is.

Reality is one and it's the same for everyone, it's the debris that make us perceive reality in a different way, but if this reality is seen from rivers that are incredibly far from the matrix, this leads to a state of a so-called *madness*: a vision of reality through one nonabsorbed debris only, which becomes a sort of replacement matrix. There are a lot of alarm bells that can induce external agents, as if attracting them, to bring help…". This is how in the 2000 I was trying to create a subconscious' architecture using the ultimate metaphor of life: the sea's flow.

The sea where everything goes, through rivers that cross mountains, hills and plains. Nature's morphology that transfers into us.

We are nature's reflection; nature, that can sometimes be abandoned and offended, and can sometimes be cured and loved. The agent is 'the other' who we reach out to but who responds to us only if he knows that our nature is as nature as its nature is.

The meaning of existence is the convergence of experiences that give us humanity's reason, they are tools that we acquire through the consciousness of the fact that seasons are not eternal and that darkness and light alternate, like hot and cold, rain and drought and this is written in every river that flows inside of us.

Emotions are the result of an internal pattern, a sort of architecture of the subconscious' fantasy where the elements are real and are the expressions of how we feel things. Poetry has the gift of making us understand how the image becomes emotion, poetry just like art in general, is simply a subconscious' representation or act.

The lack of experience is vulnerability, which often leads us to block the flow and to confuse 'the everything' with 'the particular'. This way we could perceive a cold season as life in general and the incapacity to resist takes the shape of an actual psychological disorder.

Reconnecting to nature's vitality is the path to take to get out of anxiety, starting to flow again beyond the obstacles having faith that once the cold ends this experience too will be an additional tool to fully live reality and to recognize in 'the other' a nature to respect and to protect as much as ours.

ANXIETY AND ITS SYMPTOMS

Anxiety is one of the responses that our body or our mind apply in certain situations. It's the fact of experimenting our vulnerability that often lets us understand the impossibility of handling symptoms that until that moment were lacking attention. There is a mechanism that I will call the *"mechanism of obsession"* which consists of fixing a thought without it being a fluidity of images. A sort of photography of a live image's part to which an excessive emotion is followed. It's as if in some way a themed mechanism actuates, a sort of genre, and it's being broadcasted on a loop.

There are two specific indexes that, if contained, can protect us from anguish: the first one is the *"index of vulnerability"* which is the ability to resize reality without being caught up in it or at least the more you are caught up with it the higher the vulnerability is. The second one is the *"index of obsession"* which is for how long and how often the obsessive images described above wind. If the index of vulnerability is low the images don't have any effect, we could say that repetitions are actually frequent in everyday life, if the index of vulnerability is high some sort of oppression takes over which is not fear but a feeling of helplessness and of extreme limit, the so-called angst. It's clear that a high index of obsession is a sign of discomfort that doesn't however necessarily trigger an anxiety crisis. If we experience vulnerability while deeply stressed, obsessions become a mental attempt to find answers to specific fears.

Obsessions' nature is determined by a content that always has to do with the impossibility of handling something and therefore with the fear of going insane, of dying, of being wrong, ect, ect, a sort of screening of images with dramatic content which are an exasperation of emotions symbolically represented by behaviours we suppose we can have.

A sort of dream that represents the powerlessness in front of emotions, is a dramatic representation and a representation by images of what made us experience our vulnerability.

If, for example, someone exceeds their physical strength or suffers a trauma this person experiences something that can't be controlled, this something will be replicated through obsessions' symbolic content until the index of vulnerability will not be restored. When this is acute, relax, meditation, psychotherapy could be insufficient just like it would be wrong to take medications at the first signs of vulnerability. Knowing we are strangers to that something which scares us during a panic attack is a conquest that we make after a while and that goes through a higher and higher self-awareness. Learning to reallocate obsessive thoughts in the dream's or emotion's sphere is a job that on one hand has the consequence of helping us protect ourselves from excessive fatigues and on the other hand of teaching us the ability to learn to make change more fluid. Because we are being unfair to ourselves if we are convinced that we are the image we have of ourselves. We are also what is not thought about and what is not possible to think about. We are a stream with an unknown destination, we can affect the flow but we must not interrupt it. Obsession has the characteristic of convincing us we are that thought but the thought is only a minimal part of our lives. Anxiety is just the clear proof that we are what we don't think we can be.

To make this awareness ours is to heal from vulnerability, because intimately obsession becomes an emotion and this is one of the many thrills of the adventure that is life.

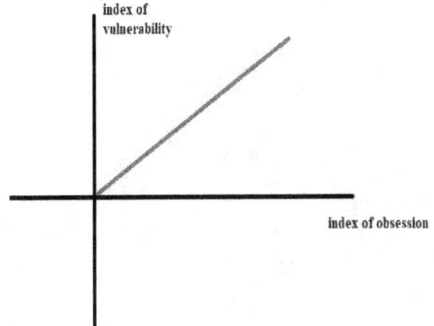

Indexes of anxiety

ANGER AS A DEFENSE FROM VULNERABILITY

Losing self-esteem and being fragile can put us in the condition of defending us from others. 'The other' becomes someone who wears us out or who uses us or who makes fun of us. Actually, is vulnerability's condition itself that leads us to defend ourselves, often improperly. With a high level of vulnerability, suggestion and perception increase. It's exactly because of this maximum alert's condition that we activate, that we often end up feeding anxiety's system.

Let's think for example about someone who's afraid of being insane: this person will be surprised at any sound or could get angry just for one glance too many as if the other could see the discomfort in him.

Vulnerability and obsession take place starting from something that is new to us. If there is something new we become more vulnerable until, through obsessing, we find the answers that we need. The anxious crisis is a void to be filled, an answer to be found that could also be a part of ourselves to take out of repression or out of devaluation. In other words anxiety is experimenting our vulnerability in front of life, a sort of deja vu of the really first moments of our existence.

THE PART FOR THE WHOLE

This balance between obsessions and vulnerability can lead to believe that obsession's meaning talks about something that is defined, in reality the symbolic meaning is prior to the trauma: what we were repressing had a reason to be repressed, for example our inability to confront or to show our true selves fearing judgement.

These emotions that arrive are often accompanied by memories of events where we suffered, what our mind selects is our pain, shrinking the picture and the most authentic reasons.

We can often come to the point where we feel hatred for a person because our mind shows us all of the times where she made us feel uncomfortable, when actually the same person has also loved us and we loved her too.

One of the things we learn the most through the journey of awareness of anxiety is that we were the one to decide back then to wear the mask and that the others played a role out of attribution.

Anxiety teaches to destroy the mask here and now, and we can remain ourselves and face who makes us feel uncomfortable even at the cost of not dedicating our time and our love to them. In the context we are a crucial piece: if we change, the whole picture changes, and anxiety hides this knowledge from us.

THE SUBCONSCIOUS IS MEMORY

Physical outer reality is recorded with a specific moment's perception. That perception belongs to an internal configuration starting from education which creates fears and concerns recorded as painful experiential paths. What we see and hurts us emotionally is a path that generates pain that can come back anytime we retrace the same path inside of us.

island

archipelago

matrix

rivers

30

The river (see '*I fiumi di Jane*') as a stream of consciousness that holds experience inside itself can dip into experiences that are distant from the matrix and can arrive to configure a common memory of experiences or islands, constituting a memory of the particular where the things we remember reappear in the mind through its process of washing the archipelago of our existence. They are moments of dread, experiences of oppression, a sense of liberation, sometimes anger, fear or immobilisation. What is clinically called anxiety is often characterised by a feeling of helplessness that is nostalgia of the matrix. A sort of stagnant force that tricks us presenting itself as matrix. Is the particular that scares us in the ghost of what is general.

IMPULSE AND ACTION

The river is a metaphor in an internal path inside the memories which translates into a behavioral manifestation. Just like our mind explores paths of memory, so we explore reality. The images that we see are the same images that are met by the mind, just like the emotions we feel respond to the same logic to which thoughts that utilise memory data respond. There is 'determination' which is responding to a focus on certain goals, there is 'obsession' which is focusing on specific thoughts' scenes, real representations on which we imagine dramatic consequences that we suppose can happen.

Thoughts observe reality's data that are also foreign to us, scenes, images, that we encountered in our everyday life. Thoughts' logics are behaviour's logics. Except, thinking is not doing, if anything it is watching. Obviously if a child sees dramatic scenes he can be shocked, just like an adult with a high level of vulnerability will be a distressed and anxious adult.

Derealization is the supposed predominance of the mind: it makes you live the impulse to do as if doing would be liberating from the thought itself, is the obsessive mechanism that, when translated to an immoral term, becomes scary. Would the impulse be that of eating it would be different!

The imperative mechanism of anxiety is actually a mechanism lacking in frustration. There is a lack of containment because the child who desires often also desires what hurts him as well, and if he's not freed from the slavery of thinking/doing he will never grasp its deepest meaning. Frustration is what creates the line between being the whole or being a part of the whole. We love in so far as we perceive the other, if the other is ourselves we fall back into the mechanism of the undefined. So if we don't create inside of us the ability to contain, frustrate, we will be scared in front of representation's bullying exactly because we will not be able to downsize it to its nature of image. Like I wrote earlier, to think is to watch, just like when you watch while you are walking.

THE DEVELOPMENT OF THE SYMPTOM

Recovery from anxiety often happens through shifting and through conviction. There is a state of vulnerability that has to be quelled by building a structure that is able to sustain experiences that are otherwise too invasive, this evolutionary step needs a transformation that goes through reliving phases of deep anxiety. The solution not to cope with anxiety and therefore the process of change, is to structure the signification of anxiety's symptoms around some syndrome. A crosscheck that gives shape to the anxious picture eases the weight of experiences of vulnerability, and the more the shape translates into a syndrome or disease, the lighter the symptoms become. So that asthma could be the cure from anxiety, as well as a presumed hernia, a rheumatic pain, a gastritis and a "weak" bowel. These "diseases" structure the perception of discomfort in a much more acceptable way and, for example, you become worried because you have asthma instead of angst, in fact angst starts to fade and becomes worry about what asthma doesn't allow to do or about the appointments with the allergist and about the treatments to cure asthma, which you will often have for your entire life... Focusing on an impulse take on similar dynamics as well, for example you become phobic in order not to feel a much deeper discomfort. The content of our thoughts recalls well-defined themes, which keep us in a state of vulnerability but that in reality are just reviving a situation in which we were too small and helpless in front of situations that were not emotionally manageable. An exercise we can do with a high level of vulnerability is to feed thoughts to our minds: in fragility's dynamic, suggestibility leads us to dwell on any subject.

THE EXASPERATED SYMPTOM

An eye-opening characteristic of people who become aware of anxiety is that they trace back the cause of their discomfort to exasperations due to the inability to handle certain frustrations.

It's like the tolerance to frustration decreases and as if the fact of not being perfect is enough to recontact vulnerability.

It's a situation of pain because a person could suffer and feel desperate just because of a remark on their look, because of a taste that is not shared by someone else or because of an opinion against that intimate desire of being approved.

Paradoxically the need is that of being fed positive and encouraging incentives, a sort of "you're always right", "you are great", exactly because this vulnerability threshold undermines self-esteem a lot. The system feeds itself if we remain stuck on the mechanism that everything has to be approved. It feeds itself because that would confirm our perpetual vulnerability.

ANXIETY'S SYSTEM

Vulnerability and obsessions are natural mechanisms that occur based on the events that we live. During anxiety the trigger mechanism is skipped: it's like we are caged in an emotion that triggers the mechanism without it being a specific stimulus. The impact with this functioning is disarming, exactly because we feel unpleasant emotions without a reason. We gradually enter anxiety's system, which means that more or less consciously we feed angst with fear or with avoidance or with compulsions. I'll explain better! Thinking we could have a crisis, we guard ourselves by avoiding places, social situations, commitments, proving ourselves that we are even more vulnerable. When the obsessive aspect shows us fears of... killing, doing something wrong, losing control, we avoid situations or stimuli that could make us kill, do something wrong, get sick ect ect, the compulsion mechanism is triggered which is the mechanism of doing something in order to prevent supposed (non-existing) risks proving us even more how vulnerable we are. The system that feeds itself is a perfect one, made to last. Is the anxiety disorder! Another thing that makes the process of getting out of anxiety difficult, is the concatenation of physical symptoms that make the state of distress a system that is feeding on itself. One of these symptoms is insomnia. Insomnia feeds the physical stress and during the day the body remains on a state of activation or of agitation. There are episodes that trigger anxiety because they recall fragility, a cover of fragility, a cover that is made of convictions of an inviolable identity. A wound to this identity leads to anger as a defensive response, attachment for an identity is already a sign of a latent fragility itself. Fragility must be accepted rather than be fixed, seen with the right instruments as if we were another person observing ourselves.

ANXIETY'S SELF-DECEPTION

Fear and escape show an analogy to shyness and to escaping someone's gaze. We are stood over, this vulnerability is the same vulnerability that makes us slaves to the stiffen thought. The images remain imprinted and they scare us exactly because they stand over us. Anxiety definitely has to do with insecurity, it has to do with the fear of being ourselves to the fullest, and only by giving up the imperative of "being someone" we are able to rebuild our identity acknowledging our right to be ourselves.

Identity doesn't become something to hide to be with others but it's something that determines our relationships and what we do instead. In this configuration, dysfunctional anxiety does not exist. Evaluation starts from recognizing ourselves, building our self-esteem on a mask is self-deception.

STIFF THOUGHTS

Stiff thoughts: thoughts that are not fluid and that sometimes can be scary.
A lot of people think that they are what they think, actually nothing is more incorrect than that. Thoughts are often fantasies. What scares us is what we would never do. These thoughts come as an attempt to ward off things we would never want to happen.
Thoughts are often symbolic representations of something we fear. Believing we could hurt someone could mean we would never tolerate this thing instead of the opposite.
Vulnerability can lead us to confuse fantasy with desire, when actually the thought which worries us is never a desire, if anything it is the obsessed desire, a part of obsession that doesn't have anything to do with what we want or what we do.
Healing from anxiety means to take off the 'cast' from the thoughts. Vulnerability often creates the fear of

losing control which can stiffen the fear of hurting others, this means that from an initial fear we end up building a second one that is nothing less than a risk based on a condition that is not real. The fear of losing control doesn't correspond to the loss of control so we often suffer because of thoughts originated from nothing. This is an example of how the obsessive mechanism can generate stiff thoughts.

Going back to the healing, to take off the cast means to let thoughts flow, we must get out of vulnerability to do so. There are two paths: confronting the traumas to which we brought the traumatic experience or reinforcing again your own self-esteem, which is reinforcing the ability to live up to the situations. These two paths often move in parallel because the increase of self-esteem is often a result of the increase of consciousness, living up to situations will basically also mean recognizing your own limits and respecting them. The stiff thought's lesson is exactly that of making us evolve in the direction of acceptance of the fact that being ourselves also means to deal with our own limits while also respecting other people's limits.

A sort of window on a human way of functioning.

RESISTANCE: THE THEME OF I DON'T WANT IT ANYMORE…

In consciousness' alteration, and therefore, inside of a high obsessive rate, when images and consciousness alter the normal perception of thoughts' flow, another important factor is resistance. Our position compared to what is happening. It's like saying that if instead of our thoughts there was a situation we didn't tolerate, we won't tolerate the thoughts the same way. What is commonly called inflexibility.

Poor tolerance to frustration often makes us more resistant to take part in certain social situations, in the same way we will pay for this resistance in a high obsessive rate.

Paradoxically, it becomes therapeutic to acquire the ability to tolerate situations avoided to get out of anxiety. The so-called intrusive and annoying images gain power exactly thanks to our intolerance. Giving less importance to certain situations is the winning attitude in order to diminish thoughts' weight. As I was writing earlier, in fact, in front of an anxious flow is just the fact of not wanting anxiety that creates the condition. The cure is to give in, not to avoid, is to learn new strategies, not to create barriers.

The symptom is a manifested resistance, is the need to create new spaces. Avoiding others and therefore avoiding situations is often actually avoiding parts of ourselves. To fear something is to fear ourselves, and 'the other' who we are afraid of is 'another' who also lives inside of us and with whom we must learn to feel good. Mental space is real space and this is also the meaning I wanted to give to the book "I fiumi di Jane".

ANXIETY AND THE EXASPERATION OF THE SYMPTOMS

One of anxiety's main characteristic is the subjective fear that takes shape, starting from a catastrophic interpretation of body symptoms.

If we have a high vulnerability to sweating, muscle rigidity, tachycardia, tingling, these could be read as signs or confirmations of our most catastrophic fears.

It's like having a board with a cartoon drew on it, a cartoon of which we have to decide the dialogues and the colours and it's like we're only having catastrophic ideas and vivid colours in mind.

The way we read our symptoms always come from our deepest fears. For example, a person who's afraid of being insane could read muscle rigidity as a presence or as an hallucination and someone who believes to be sick could read tachycardia as a heart attack, and so on similar symptoms are seen in a subjective way with the constant of an imminent catastrophe.

ANXIETY AND ONE'S OWN LIFE STORY

One of the most important signals about the fact we are reworking what we have repressed is exactly the fact that we feel distressed when recalling images of our life story. Images that remind us of how we "decided to overlook it" and of how we were "doing things anyway" when there actually were all of the reasons to feel distressed. The angst we were feeling then, we relive it right now and reliving that angst is actually a signal we are getting out of anxiety, even if it may seem like a hard relapse during the process of healing. A child can't process really strong emotions like experiences of neglect or abuse as an adult can. If anxiety shows up when we are adults, it's simply sending us the message we should get back that authentic part of ours that we put aside as a "magic" strategy to not be abandoned or abused. Reliving past anguishes is the first step to reconnect to our true identity.

Vulnerability often leads us to protect ourselves from that anguish though. Framing facts and events well makes us more confident. If anxiety shows up today it's because we need that repressed part, if the brain sends us that repressed anguish it's because it evaluated that we are able to handle it. To trust nature is one of the elements that is devalued by the anxious person. It's like we want to control even nature and like we can't trust anyone. It's classic hearing from someone who suffers from anxiety that they would like to escape even their own self. When we run away from ourselves we run away from something that we are afraid of expressing, which is the part that made us suffer in the past and that we decided to delete because we considered it to be responsible for our pain.

He who fantasized as a child to be abandoned or to not be wanted could be extremely available and take care of other people's problems when he becomes an adult, only to later feel even more abandoned and misunderstood, unconsciously feeding a system of insecurity and of not having self-confidence. During a moment of extreme stress these people will definitely reconnect with vulnerability, going through anxiety will give them the possibility to be able to live the relationships with others peacefully and without feeling guilty in an equal situation.

We can lower our level of vulnerability only by regaining our self-esteem and this transition starts from the integration of those emotions or behaviours that were repressed to not be abandoned or to be loved.

We deserve to be loved without conditioning, if someone threatens us they only do it because they want to control us!

It's we who decide how much time to spend with them. Little children can live a threat from someone as a full on reality, for example if the mom tells to the young son that if he doesn't eat she doesn't want him anymore the child could think: "I must eat or else mom will abandon me"... which is transformed into "mom would have abandoned me because I wasn't eating, imagine if I make her mad or I make disasters, etc etc...", in a spiral of anxieties that the brain will wrap and give us back when we become adults. Children live anxiety too, but they often don't have the ability to contain themselves so a lot of thoughts get repressed by our brain because of a spirit of self-preservation which is the same principle to why we should trust our body's nature.

A lot of adults somatize because they are not ready to hold the weight of anguish, therefore nature can send them anguishes back through digestive difficulties or migraine. Anxiety is an undefined disquiet, a feeling of apprehension and danger! A confirmation of the impossibility to heal. It's desperation, obsession, fragility but also a lack of balance, tachycardia, hyperventilation, sweating and blurred vision.

Muscle rigidity and fear of... killing, being wrong, getting sick and not making it. It's an announced disaster but also an incredible insightful adventure, a possibility to comprehend others and ourselves, the only road to be free from conditioning and from masks that we wore for years, often without being aware of it. It's a liberation that comes at a high price , an incredible chance to become ourselves!

The process of healing goes just through all of this.

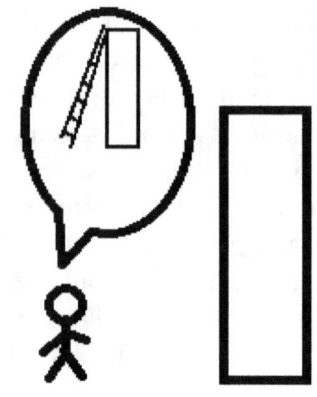

Scheme of loss

THE SCHEME OF LOSS

The person is vulnerable in front of a wall that seems insurmountable, we can feel violent and desperate so the thought (the obsession) tries to find even magic, symbolic solutions; it could meet witches, deads. The "staircase" solution takes place starting from a change inside of us that leads us to be confident about our ability in making it, starting from recognizing that part of ourselves that is convinced of the opposite. It seems like anxiety is a comparison with something huge that inevitably meets a similar past experience. A person who's convinced of not being important enough and worthy of love can try to supplant this thought by filling their lives with objects (job, friends, commitments, interests, classes), this action of filling is effective only until we don't experience the inability to make it again.

The solution could be that of recognizing our right to be loved and lovable by setting parts of ourselves that we traded for love free. In fact, it often happens that the compromise to be loved when we were children is exactly that of being liked, giving up desires and spontaneity which are often actual repressed talents.

The mind is a thunder

The mind is a thunder
with a frightening rumble
with echoes of images
that stake naked walls
of fragility.
After the storm
there is nothing left
of a sun kissed
field of flowers,
when we are hanging
on anchors of fear…
When we are suspended
between the cracking earth
and a flying seagull...

EXPERIENCES OF ABANDON/SEPARATION

Who suffers from anxiety can experience the fear of being alone, an anguish that seems to resemble the one children show when their mom leaves them in the arms of a stranger or crying in a crib.

The anguish that comes from abandon, a sort of desperation associated to an uncontainable fear. A very high gradient of vulnerability even without obsessions makes us children in diapers, symbiotic beings who are not enough for themselves to survive.

It seems like there is an increasing lack of self-confidence, which confirms the inability to handle ourselves or to handle anguish depending on how we want to look at it.

ANALYSIS OF THE ORIGINS

Since life itself is a collection of events that make our ability to tolerate frustration come into play, we need to find the common thread of traumatic events in anxiety. In order to bring obsession back to its emotional condition we need to work backwards, therefore we need to understand how this emotion, that has been held down, becomes obsession when facing the stressful event. In other words, we need to understand the causes of this emotion, and also understand its context and function as well. We often have anger that we repress not to feel it, we please and try to be liked by everyone, the stressful event increases our vulnerability, and obsession brings anger into play. Anger doesn't have anything to do with anxiety but if we want to improve our condition we need to also look at the reason why we have it. Finding the origin guides us towards a change of our entire personality. So to sum it up, the fears of going crazy, doing something wrong, dying, etc etc, are linked to vulnerability; obsessive fantasies are linked to the emotions we used to repress before the traumatic event.

We feel the change when we realize that situations that were normal before, now become too tight for us because we are retrieving our right to always be our authentic selves.

The person who wasn't expressing their anger when they were receiving impositions from certain figures, for example from parents, will start to feel the discomfort and the right to defend themselves.

SELF ESTEEM AND THE THEORY OF ONE'S SELF

Vulnerability is an unpleasant and distressing condition, to use a metaphor it's like being a snail on a busy sidewalk or paradoxically a bystander that can crush someone without realizing it.

The metaphor obviously represents the psychological experiences and not what we are actually going to do. Experiences that were so scary that they often generate the fear of reliving them, so that they become a problem themselves. Vulnerability could paradoxically feed itself with confirmations of fragility.

To heal our self-esteem we need to water the sprout that we have inside, we need somehow to grow starting from our authenticity. The most extreme need of a young child is to have adults as their alleys exactly because the adult who is so big and tough can be nice but also mean and threatening. The child will adapt to the requests even if it means to give up on being himself. It is common, and sadly it works very well, to threaten your own children in order to make them more obedient.

A threat could be for example: "if you do this you will make mommy cry... if you cry I don't want you anymore, etc etc...". My description of childhood is just an attempt to make the reader recall all of the images that have to do with this scheme in adulthood. Being fragile also means being easily manipulated and feeling guilty. This justifies abuses often accepted in a couple or in a work context as a sort of death (very common as a theme in the early days of anxiety through dreams or symbolic thoughts) of the old life in exchange for a new one. Rebirth brings us back to the scheme of vulnerability and here, going back to what I wrote about the sprout earlier, it's up to our rational part to take care of it.

Healing is relation and realization, it's coming into contact with the things that make us feel better even if we think we are not able to.

It's a revolution of our beliefs about ourselves, a rediscovery of our ethic.

INDEX

5. *ANXIETY*

7. PRESENTATION

13. INTRODUCTION

19. ANXIETY AND ITS SYMPTOMS

23. <u>INDEXES OF ANXIETY</u>

25. ANGER AS A DEFENCE FROM VULNERABILITY

27. THE PART FOR THE WHOLE

29. THE SUBCONSCIOUS IS MEMORY

32. IMPULSE AND ACTION

35. THE DEVELOPMENT OF THE SYMPTOM

37. THE EXASPERATED SYMPTOM

39. ANXIETY'S SYSTEM

41. ANXIETY'S SELF-DEPICTION

42. STIFF THOUGHTS

45. RESISTANCE: THE THEME OF I DON'T WANT IT ANYMORE...

47.   ANXIETY   AND   THE
EXASPERATION   OF   THE
SYMPTOMS
49. ANXIETY AND ONE'S OWN
LIFE STORY
54. <u>THE SCHEME OF LOSS</u>
55. THE SCHEME OF LOSS
57. *THE MIND IS A THUNDER*
58.   EXPERIENCES   OF
ABANDON/SEPARATION
59. ANALYSIS OF THE ORIGIN
61. SELF-ESTEEM AND THE
THEORY OF ONE'S SELF

www.ingramcontent.com/pod-product-compliance
Lightning Source LLC
Chambersburg PA
CBHW070321290526
45791CB00003B/1203